Shagufta K Iqbal is an artist working
theatre and film. She has performec
Literature Festival, Bloomsbury Litera
Festival, Birmingham MAC and Brist

Shagufta has been performing ar
several years, and has studied Engl
Studies at Bath Spa University, and has a master... ....
Studies.

She is interested in bringing poetry to a wider audience,
particularly through the use of spoken word, and live theatre.
Keen to merge activism with art, she is a powerful and brave
voice. A prime example of this is her 2015 poetry film *Borders*,
with director Elizabeth Mizon, which has been screened at
London Short Film Festival, Encounters Film Festival, Tongues
on Fire- London Asian Film Festival, and Underwire Film Festival.

Jam Is for Girls, Girls Get Jam

Shagufta K Iqbal

Burning Eye

BurningEyeBooks
Never Knowingly
Mainstream

This edition published by Burning Eye Books 2017

www.burningeye.co.uk

@burningeyebooks

Burning Eye Books
15 West Hill, Portishead, BS20 6LG

ISBN 978-1-911570-00-4

Elspeth,
Thank you for listening to
the words, hope you enjoy
Love + Light

[signature]

Jam Is for Girls,
Girls Get Jam

CONTENTS

THE LAUGH OF THE MEDUSA

Dedicated to my grandmothers.

My maternal grandmother
was known for her fire.
My paternal grandmother
was known for her silences.

Language was not constructed
to roll off our tongues.
It was not made to ease
the suffering of women.
To contextualise our pain.

We gave birth to our own expression.
We bore our own conversations.

Through fire and silence I hear it.
Through fire and silence I understand.
Through fire and silence come our stories.

RIVER AVON

JAM IS FOR GIRLS, GIRLS GET JAM

But we awoke to the sizzle of eggs in the pan.
I like mine well done
and my sister liked hers with the yolk just so.
Yes, we were girls, yet we got eggs, not jam.

But. We were made to know:
I was not born boy,
I was not born to be man,
I was born to be given away
and that's why girls get jam.
And that is why I have not one
but three beautiful sisters.
Because I was not born boy.

And I was made to know that:
I escaped the desert sands,
my mouth was not placed over with hand.
I was lucky enough to be born after the gift of the Qur'an,
to be protected by the word of Allah.
And still my *Ummah* does not hear
the compassion bestowed upon us by Allah,
Still my *Ummah* chooses not to see
the light bestowed upon us by Allah.

Yes, bones lie scattered
criss-crossing through the deserts
under the feet of our beloved prophets.
And like my mother the desert heat suppresses secrets,
and mass graves gather under sand dunes.
No, I cannot tell you why that girl child,
buried breathing, lies in the embrace of the Sahara.

And yes, I must cover.
Live enshrouded.
Black cloth grazing against my skin,
protecting me from everyone else's sin.
My face, my eyes, my lips, my words and my honesty.
And yet I must pluck, and wax, and squeeze, and polish, and lipo,
and smile, full lips, big tits, designer vagina.
Because this way it gets called freedom.
You see, my identity and my honour lie not in me,

12

but in those who own me,
and oh, how they adorn me.
I tinsel like Christmas tree.
Purple bruises sparkle against my face.
Because in the land of the free,
by the man I love,
I am battered every fifteen seconds,
and in the land of democracy
I was only given the right to speak in 1918
'Shhhhhhhh, yes,' he said, 'husssssssssssh,'
because only in 1991 did it become rape.
So 'Don't say a word,' he says.
But I, I've just got to ask, is that why even today
only 4.2% of rape cases lead to conviction in Bristol?
Yes, they all just let him walk away.

Because I was not born boy,
I was not born to be man.
I was born to be given away.
And that's why girls get jam.

And like traitors they say we give away land,
we do not carry on our fathers' names,
we disappear in family trees,
no one can trace who we are,
there is no leaf left for me.
And silent as sweltering nights,
we are considered to have come from thin air.
Giving birth to strong sons,
serving great husbands,
and burning to death on funeral pyres.
The Ganges just rolling on by,
unperturbed by that smell of burning flesh,
that stench of charred hair,
that one tumbled down a honey-brown back.

And they remind us
that we got lumbered with jam,
we were born to be given away
and no one loves those
who aren't here to stay.

FIVE POUNDS

What we have here is the energy
that comes from a mix of races,
those faces from all over places,
the hunger to do better in the motherland.

Villages left behind,
prayers and wishes
hanging over the five rivers,
'Do for you,
and then remember us
and do for us,' they hoped.
They kissed palms
and, forehead to forehead,
imprinted memories.
Whole villages rallied round,
gathered up airfares,
sent men with suitcases
and only a £5 note
to go make futures.
You sent sons and daughters
into downpours of rain,
and under hazy heat we've lost you.
Your face sits foggy in our collective memories.
The images of you are jagged, and torn, and blinked away.

STOP AND SEARCH

You see it was these streets,
this neighbourhood that shaped and formed us.
In summers we sunshined in the carnival,
and it took a while for the Pakistanis
that lived side by side
with the Afro-Caribbean community
to sit stalls side by side in the July heats.
A once-only jerk chicken, curry goat, dumpling & rice and peas
    menu opened up.
Carnival started becoming a money maker for everyone,
samoseh sold, pakoreh sold, channa sold,
the local authority jumped in,
set up its red tape and counted its notes.

My mum stopped worrying
about the early mornings
where she would find drunken men
sleeping off rum-soaked dreams
on our garden wall.

And, yes, there was poverty.
In the spring of 1980
my mum would tight shut doors
against the aftermath
of stop and search abuse.
The most raided premises
in the country
at the heart of it,
the black and white café,
is where racial tension came to a head.

It wasn't so much our problem back then,
that everyday hate and discrimination
that was so ingrained in Thatcher's impoverished Britain.
We were just Pakis back then,
kept our head down,
got our work done,
and got out when the time was right.

We were Muslims,
but we shared our commonality
instead with Hindus and Sikhs,
we were Desis.
We knew nothing about
the Arabi or Somali back then.

We kept our head down,
got our work done,
we didn't rise up,
it wasn't our riot,
it wasn't our problem back then.

And for hours my mother
would watch the riot rolling
its force through her streets,
police chiefs adamant,
'Surely we should be advancing, not retreating.'

The shortest motorway in the country
cut one of the most deprived areas
of Bristol in two.
And it watched with indifference
at the smashed cars
and fires blazing,
at Black power
being led away in handcuffs.

CIRCLING THE CITY

The sting of cigarette smoke,
men sat on tired chairs,
iron and flat foam.
Bottoms that ached from
twelve-hour taxi shifts.
Grey clouds surrounded their
heads like the Sufi's beard.
Beads of sweat glistened on foreheads,
and the lime-green walls themselves
were made of candle wax.
Trousers were rolled up to the knees,
and shirt sleeves freeing the hot
skin from cottoned constraint.

Once these men had rivers
running through their limbs.
These men, experts in guiding
the ebb and flow of whole cities.
Their lives a journey
of pick-ups and drop-offs.
Etched in their blood the
track of railroads;
deep in their bones,
cargo and destinations;
at the back of their hands,
maps of adopted homes,
and in the memories
of their fingertips,
the faint ghost of homelands.

STOKES CROFT

Yup, they always send in the hippies first,
all love, no war, all theory.
It's alright when poor sods are staring at you
from TV screens and magazines
with trauma-vacant eyes.
But here, suddenly no one can see
what's straight up under their nose.

And you get poverty living side by side
with the cool, the eclectic and edgy.
The make-up of these streets
has changed up.
And beard wearers,
tight trousers hugging,
hipster heads
bob their way down these pavements.
And, yes, essentially we are all just consumers,
but nowhere near this level,
we can't match them in this.
Because they buy out identities
and appropriate cultures
like disposable high street fashions.
Yes, they consume us around here,
cultures are cooked up and devoured.
Samosas without the Indians,
hummus without the Palestinians,
jerk without the Jamaicans.

Once a friend noted how safe it is here.
'It's all changed,' she said.
True, it's all changed,
it's safe.
It's safe for you,
safe of mes.
Yes, you like the people of places,
skin colours like rainbows gleaming down these streets.
Yes, you like the people of places,
but *only*, only when they're being useful,
like nodding their heads
in 'Rice & Peas'

and 'Curry & Kebab.'
Nodding from behind counters,
nodding from behind kitchen doors,
nodding, nodding, always nodding
Yes, *masa* sir and *gee hah shahib*,
no problem *shahib*.

Watch, Easton
will follow the same suit.
Give it time.
Shoreditch and Whitechapel
have already paved our path.

It's called the John Cabot effect,
the Merchants' Quarter effect
the Colston's effect.
It's called the get 'em out,
move 'em on effect.

And regeneration,
regeneration happened
side by side with community cuts.
No more Kuumba,
no more CEED,
no more Humdard,
they weren't fit for function.
Our support systems demolished,
and our lives packed up.

We're strewn round here for decorative purposes only.
No one will reach out with words and strike up conversations.
Two worlds side by side as if in parallel universes.
Yes, like light-years-away stars.
We're strewn round here for decorative purposes only.
So shhhhhh, twinkle, and just look the part.

RAPUNZEL

My mother worried she would have to raise her children here.

We, on the other hand, were oblivious,
because on sticky concrete summer days
I remember lying on the school's red pitch
and watching the waves of heat dance
upwards, off the soft gravelled ground:
ground that imprinted into my skin
like a kiss leaving behind goosebumps.
A playground that shrunk in size,
swallowed up,
folded into the vertical climb of our inner city.

Where colour and politics bled off the walls
and stamped themselves into my memory,
floating declarations of *I waz ere*
battling against the city's ability to swallow
individuals and their existence.
We got eaten up, chewed up and spat out.
Zombies started walking our streets,
crack had a free rein.
And half-empty cans would sit on garden walls
spreading that stale smell of grapes,
enticing the already hammered flies.

And after school between the sounds
of incessant sirens we would listen out
for the chimes of the ice cream van
that would brave itself onto our streets.
We would drop our world at its arrival
and with the neighbouring children
chase down its promises, with sweaty
palm-clutched pocket money.
Running amidst the dusty shadows of streets,
where guns are held over uniformed black and white.

And all the while she sat up there,
a Pakistani Rapunzel
on her window sill,
her hair hanging in colourful *parandeh*.

Sometimes she watched us, but on most
days she just looked out over our heads into
the brick-layered horizon beyond
and simply soundtracked my summer
afternoons with nostalgic *qawwali*.

Even then I knew what she was waiting for.
And I held on to her disappointment as if it were my own.

AFTER THE WATERSHED

Before I grew up and before I moved,
I was still young and lived back in BS2.
And on some nights I would hear
the sounds of reggae from next door,
songs that brought out a sunshine
in the middle of the night.
You see, it was the voice of that
far-away island would put me to sleep.

Or the sounds of longing would fill my room.
Zion would creep into my dreams.
I would capture Babylon and all its rivers
in that hot continent,
and let them free in erratic colours as I slept.

But on other nights, on other nights
I would hear her screams.
Screams that came deep,
deep down, from the cracking of bones.
Her voice would reach out
through the walls
and beg for it to stop.
I would feel the blues and purples
that would splatter against her skin.
So that she would look like a sugar and a plum, plum, plum.
And I would listen, lying tucked up in bed,
to the sounds of thumps
that fell down upon her,
like the sound of a constant drum.
And she would sing out her pain to me like a lullaby
as I would drift off –
and suddenly
be woken up from sleep.
My ears would ache
listening to the silence that would follow,
where there isn't exactly silence.
Something is there.
Something is waiting to be let free,
into the air,

into our fears,
into the house next door.

Then, then I would dream shadows,
elongated, misshapen, distorted.
I would envisage a room, not unlike my own.
But a place where pain would curl itself up
and look like a sugar and a plum, plum, plum.

Her pleas would become screams,
her screams would become cries,
her cries would become lonesome sobs,
until eventually there was nothing.
Except our heavy steady breathing
separated by those thin paper walls.

And I would dream of a brown girl
skipping across the ocean,
back to that river,
back to Zion.
Back to that place called home.
But she never left him.
She stayed and she stayed and
she showed me her motion,
and she stayed and sang to me a lullaby,
night after night, after night,
of a brown girl skipping across the ocean.

RIVER SUTLEJ

SAVED

We do not speak enough
of denying our truths,
for their freedoms,
of our loyalty to our men.

And they in turn
speak too much
of how they protect us.

From what,
I do not know.
But they watch something
of themselves in shadows.
Try hard to hold its burning at bay.
Convince us we have been saved.

Yes, we have a false sense
of loyalty to our men.
We protect them from themselves.

THE MOON

There is something about the moon, he says.
I burn with rage.
There is something about the moon.
She never looks the same,
always reinventing herself.
The way she is reborn.
Fad diets,
the curves,
bones,
curves,
bones.
And in that darkness I drown, he cries.
A lifeless body, floating amongst the entangling seaweed.
I am caught.
The night skies bear down on me.
The light of the moon always out of reach.
The stars glowing their smugness.
Rage. I feel it build up in my chest.
I untangle myself.
Reach out instead for the brightness of the sun,
swallow its beams through my mouth,
through my throat,
and let it explode light out through my chest.
I want to burn.
Enshadow that moon.
Stop the waves in their adoration,
turn the tides back.
Stop that blood flow,
its ability to breathe life.
There is something about that moon.
How she is reborn.
I burn with rage.

SELKIE

She is not an Irish myth.
She looks at her skin
and it is real.
Her womb heavy,
full with the decisions of others.
She is real.
She watches her body,
and knows it is not hers anymore.
She used to spend all her time
with her body in the water,
slipping beneath its slicing surface.
Breathing in another world.
Yes, sometimes she feels she was born of sea.
It was easy to almost curl into it.
To almost let it take you.

It took the weight off her feet,
the burden off her mind.
Her skin would almost wrinkle-crinkle.
Light. Almost weightless.
Her womb in her hands,
almost quietened.
Almost.
Almost.
Her pregnancy could almost have stayed a secret.
Almost.
Almost.
She could have almost slowed time right down, almost.
But like a net the 24th week lies in wait in the not-too-far
distance.
All tangle. All coarse. All skin burn and noose.

She has become used to not recognising her own body.
As it grows month by month.
Wishing will not bring it to an end.
Wishing will not give her body back.

And she holds her breath
as the decision makers
steal her skin,

bones,
limbs
with the eighth amendment
tearing into her.
Prodded and poked.
Stretch marks tighten their grip
around her memories of violences,
violations.
Manhandled and broken.
Silvered scars.
C-shaped anchor,
grinning across landwrecked skin.
Her body sits on her bones haphazardly.
Like a phantom limb it pushes down on her.
Despite being cut and pulled and stitched back together,
she still feels like pieces,
scattered across seashelled beaches.
Pebble-ingrained skin unrecognisable.
The water doesn't work its magic anymore.
Each crash of each wave that lands at her feet
reminds her that her soul is anchored where it should not be.
And no amount of looking out to sea will set her free.
Not while they keep snapping her body into so many pieces.

MINERVA SULIS

'I let him touch me,'
she says.
Lips red bright,
nails dark blue,
as she slips a cigarette into my palm.
Tobacco heavy in my hands,
I suddenly feel complicit in her abuse.
Like what's been stolen from her
collects like raindrops around us
as we shelter behind the school Portakabins.
Her family bonds make me shift weight in my Nikes.
The way they just take from her
as if she exists only between her lips and her legs.

'Like, don't worry.
I can get more cigarettes from him, like, whenever.'
She shrugs.
She tries to blow smoke like a star.
All wrong, pointed, angled, sharp.
With each drag she
sucks her truths in through her teeth.
Folds them away into the pit of her stomach.

I've told the teachers
about the currency of her body.
I anticipate tsunamis.
I wait.
Nothing happens.

I'm learning early on
that fourteen-year-old girls
with lips too bright,
skin too dark
will not be saved.
Because bodies like hers are made for violence.
Dark skin, supposedly, is good at concealing bruises.
Only I can see how she lives submerged under scars and pain.
And in dreams I wreak revenges on her behalf,
like gathering lost minds into my hand,
eyeballs collate like coral reefs in my silent rage.

30

But my futile violences bubble a dull echo
against the surface of the world.
We don't get heard.

And she, red-lip smiling,
watches up at us.
Yes, sometimes she just, like, studies me.
Watches the words sit like drought
between the two of us.
I can only look at her
and wish on her.

Like prayers written in code,
prayers pushed into gaps in stone walls,
tucked away into desk drawers,
prayers that won't be unearthed
until lifetimes too late.
And even then no one will find her,
and even then no one will find her childhood.
And I can only look upon her, and wish on her.

LOVE

When he pulls the childhood
our of your hair, a tight tug
against your skull, it is love.
When he shouts you
across the street, it is love.
And because he can swim, you drown,
and because he can kick, you curl,
and he goes right ahead
and grabs you by the pussy.

And when you are found,
buried in gardens,
plastic-wrapped at the bottom of lakes,
dismembered and strewn across forests,
cobwebbed and earth-ridden,
know it is love.

When your eyes tell stories
of wars and mountains,
gaping caves
where once there was a nose,
acid-drenched skin,
scars that retell
how you were pinned down,
and clumsily
one ear
then another
was sliced from you.

You will learn, child, that this too is love.
We wear the attention of men forever on our skin.

SONG

My mother's throat would sing,
guttural as *qawwali* crescendoing,
like Nusrat Fateh Ali Khan into late nights.
My neighbour's skin taut like drum
would vibrate thumps through our walls.
The lady across the road would silently hum
her bruises away in the afternoon sunshine.

Once I saw him hold her by her throat,
all sound escaping
from the roundness of her body.

I stopped knowing them by their names.
I only recognised them by their sounds.
And they sang their songs lonely,
and they sang their songs in tune with one another.

To this day, even as a grown woman,
I sometimes feel like a stupid pop song.
Unable to balance the boundaries
of love exploitation.
I know how to scream,
rage gathers in me like frenzy.
Calmness, calmness
is not readily available
in the music of my bones.

I HAVE BECOME THE THIRD PERSON I WILL BE

I once came here when I was my first self.
Young, she fell into the skies.
She was the cloud that swam
across to places unknown.
She trusted the air.
He carried her across
patchwork lands of gold,
and bright fields of rice stalks,
and reverberating grasses
that fought under the crushing of the sun.

He carried her over the waters of the Naré,
mountains that looked like timeless
islands in a sea of cloud.
Below the snow slowly gathered.
And she left behind the land of *um*,
where she would climb to the foot of that mountain range
and eat *bare*, her mouth would
open the vulnerable wet flesh of the fruit.

I can taste them in her dreams.
But she is lost to us.
Her memory, a kiss:
bruised and bloodstained
onto the softness of my skull.

But today I shall start afresh.
Not like her daughter did.
Not like my second self did.
She feared.
She twisted and entwined.
She grew her roots in strange soil.
She is tree of life,
indented with creeper vines,
stretch marks snuggled against her.
The thickness of her root anchoring her soul here.

She longs for something deeper

in the moist darkness of earth.
But she has no companion.
And grey veins of smoke suffocate the air.
No familiar jasmine settles at her feet.
Here, she soaks up the constant murmur of rain.
The wetness releases an earthy smell:
that smell of loneliness.
And she holds on to mistrust,
its memory remains with her,
like bruises bloodstained
onto the softness of my skull.

But I am now my third self.
I am not of land.
I am not of sky.
I am an elusive nomad.
But I know no more than you do
of the memory I will leave behind.
Only that I shed skins,
I leave behind ancestral tribes,
continents, gold-bordered dresses,
blood stained onto the softness of silk,
henna patterns resonant of tree limbs that
branch out against the restlessness of my hands.
I spill out into the world.
I feel it over my skin.
Like a great wave,
it splashes over me and settles into my soul.

RIVER BEAS

MEDUSA'S RAGE

It's not an invitation.
If I walk out, shoulders cinnamon-brown bare.
It's not an invitation for you to call me out
with a disrespectful great British gentleman's club shout,
voice hidden from behind your boys,
lion-loud and leering but only in crowds.

You make me wear my anger like thunderclouds.
And when I pass by and I got my red dress on,
hair long wavy sun-bleached serpentine,
suddenly you forget that this space is mine.
Suddenly you feel the need to disempower and undermine.
Sexual politics need to be redefined,
because it seems you're always crossing the line.
This space is mine.

It's not an invitation.
It's not an invitation for you to violate my personal space,
like some pervert extraordinaire.
And I feel that there is violence
in your words, it hangs in the air.
Suffocates me, it's hard for me to bear.
It makes me want to strike you down where you stand.
Backhand.
Make you understand
that if you gaze on my face I will turn you to stone.

It's not an invitation when your every word
makes me want to break your every bone.
Stop tripping over your testosterone,
take some responsibility for your actions.
The female sex is not just a distraction.

'Fatal attraction.
Her skirt was too short,
she shouldn't have been drunk,
she shouldn't have been out at this time.
Of course shit happens.
Doesn't she know boys will be boys?'

No, she doesn't.
Because having a dick is not an excuse
for this kind of abuse.
I warn you now,
these streets are mine.
I'm not going to run and hide.
I'm going to walk down real mean,
remind you that I am a queen.
I shouldn't be hearing anything obscene.

You see, our streets,
our streets are already littered with statues of men,
and I don't mind adding a few more.
Because this is not something I'm going to ignore.
I'm ready for this war.
I will stare you down and turn you to stone.

Next time you see me walking down the street,
be discreet,
accept your defeat,
you and your dick
need to retreat.
Because this,
this is not an invitation.

EXCUSE ME, MY BROTHER

Excuse me, my brother,
excuse me,
can I ask you,
can I ask you why your dress is not more Islamic?
Why is your *sootan* not way up here, my brother?
Come here, my brother, come here,
let me measure this beard you have growing,
it still looks a bit prepubescent,
not very Islamic, my brother, not very Islamic,
And tell me, why is your *khuchi* on display, my brother?
In fact, while I have your attention
and the right to discuss your body,
let me ask you,
just how circumcised is your dick, my brother?

Oh, I'm sorry, are my questions embarrassing you?

How does it feel to be told you don't measure up
to my understanding and requirements
of what it means to be Islamic enough?
That your angles and curves will be laid bare
to my judgement of how wrong you are?
That somehow through all these physical attributes
I can see into your heart, weigh up your *niat*?

Mmmnhmnn, mmmhmmmnn,
sure, outspokenness
is not very feminine, not very Islamic.
Clearly the female voice is far too alluring,
I need to shhhhhhh my heartfelt pourings.
Tones smooth and drip with honey,
and onomatopoeias that are deliberately arousing.
My assonances dance to the flutter of my eyelashes,
as playful as chimes in the wind;
they indecently beckon you, obviously.
My laugh, like soft fingertips
running over your spine, penetrates you.
And of course the explicit way my hair billows in the breeze
is an affront to all that is good and pure in this world.

Wake up, my brother. Yes, I said wake up.

Let me tell you,
it's all about context,
not always about sex.
So, my brother,
avert your gaze,
hands off my body,
and don't think you can judge my *niat*.

Listen to my words,
see me beyond the vessel
that carries my soul and mind.
Hear me. Hear me. Hear me.

THE INBETWEEN

My name was decided before the prayer in my ear.
The honey in my mouth.
The *li la ha illil la ho Muhammad ar rasullila*,
the first words I hear.
The *bismillah ah rahman neera heem*,
in the name of the most merciful, the most kind I begin,
the *li la ha illil la ho Muhammad ar rasullila*,
the last words I will breathe.
The *bismillah ah rahman neera heem*,
in the name of the most merciful, the most kind I end.

But I keep forgetting the inbetween.

'Yes, *inshallah*,' they said, 'her name is decided.'
They thought names anchor us here.
It is thought that names carry tribes,
and clans and ancestries.
Linking you to your past,
it is thought that names speak destinies.
They speak of the *Kaleh Phar*,
they speak of the rivers Punjab,
they speak of a home that is too far.

But what they didn't know is that names change.
Because before I started my name was Shabana.

Yes, destinies change,
and I have gotten used to Shagufta,
mismatched. Misspelt. Misunderstood.
We have learnt to accept the feel of one another,
the way the sssssssssssssilence
and the guttural *g*, that real hard Punjabi *g*,
yes, the fierceness,
and that *t*,
how it hits home my presence here.

Shagufta, Shagufta,
ambiguous. Nationless. Mongrelised.
It baffles immigration officers,
no one quite knows where it has come from.
No, no one quite knows where I have come from.

And I pray I don't forget it.

Because sometimes my hope falters,
my faith weakens,
I forget how to make my destiny,
mother tongues suffocate,
syllable rhythms too late,
vowels go tumbling, mixing destiny with fate,
letter patterns mispronunciate,
and the whispered prayer in my ear
and the tangle in my mind can't quite relate.
And those tribes, clans, and ancestries
don't quite correlate,
and I lose myself,
I lose my way.

Alhamdo Lillahi Rabbil Aalameen Ar Rahmaanir Raheem
Maaliki Yaomid Deen iyya Kana Budoo Wa iyya kanastaeen
ihdinas Siratual Mustaqeem Siratual Lazeena An Amtaa Alaihim
Ghairil Maghdoobe Alaihim Walad Dualleen
Ameen.

I pray, I pray,
I pray in my mongrel Arabic,
Punjabi undercutting each syllable,
and my Englishness smoothing over
my mispronounced inaccuracies.
I pray in my Potwari Arabic.
So that I know where I am going
I pray,
so that I hear that *t*.
'Cause every now and then
I gotta let it wake my soul up,
wake up,
take off this make-up,
speak up,
take up my prayer,
follow it through,
and plant my feet here.

Shagufta. Shagufta.
Bismillah ah rahman neera heem.
Don't let me get lost in the inbetween.

43

TRUTH

I wrote this poem for every time
I turned pages in *Asiana* magazine
and was confronted by skin-lightening products.
I wrote this poem for every time I switched on
BBC 1Xtra and BBC Asian Network,
and it was all light-skinned girl and *goriya veh*.
I wrote this poem when *Diya* magazine
quietly enveloped into my home,
my letterbox revealing how Indian models
were replaced with European ones.
I wrote this poem when Kajol made
a comeback with Dilwale,
her Frida Kahlo self-acceptance
now a heavy white cloud
on a once-sunny day.

I wrote this poem when I was nine,
and my sister's defiance
was held together by
the brownness of her skin.
I wrote this poem
when I looked into my daughter's face
and folded away lies into my hands,
held instead a mirror to her skin.
Showed her she is her foremothers.
Showed her she is her ancestors.
Showed her she is her goddesses.
Showed her she is
the living energy of the sun.
Showed her she is truth,
and truth is courage,
and courage is beauty,
and beauty is her.

RIVER RAVI

BOTH LIFE AND DEATH

Understand.
Jissam.
Men of Punjab,
sons of landowners and seafarers,
Aurat aur pani na keh farq.

I BOUGHT CACTI

He said they were easy to maintain.
So this time last year, I bought two:
one for you, and one for myself.

Eventually I forgot their names,
the cacti almost died soon after.

As you never took yours, I watered them
and placed them in the misty bathroom.
Your cactus sprouted an orange head
that grew tall from its rubber leaves,
and its plaited body stood proud

at first. Then it browned,
its corners curled,
and it started to fall apart.
Its water suddenly dried out.

And Mum said a sort of plant infection
had begun to grow at its root.
Just as she predicted,
a grey soft ball curled around the base,
and the cactus's colour broke free,
nothing but dying rubber leaves remained.

When yours died I gave up on the other.
In time, it too began to wilt.
Sat next to the bath,
absorbing the magnified sun,
drenched in a steamy haze,
it did not respond.

Months later, only by chance did I notice
it had grown pretty pink flowers once more,
like those you would find
on a honeysuckle bush.
Its square leaves stretched out
in every which direction.
And on the tips of the leaves fuchsia
balls wept into silky vibrant petals.

QURBANI

It is a place of darkness, always midnight.
You step in and forget what is outside.
But light pieced together like pain
is just a step to my right.
And against the red hot mud wall
is the water pump.
And the emerging droplets
that grow beams of light within.

Above me is a sound of
madness in the dark.
Its feathered flapping sends
an unnerving feel to my ears.
Nesting in the darkness of roof,
occasionally the madness releases
a heavy raindrop, that smacks
hard against the cobbled ground.
A part of the insanity,
one at a time, falls free,
flying gracefully downwards,
and pecks at the seeds
in my small warm hands.
Like moths their brown
forms illuminate in the dark,
spotlights of greens and blues
casting further shadows.

A calf next to me marks
movements anchored to the ground.
It circles around the wooden barn doors before us.

Behind them I can taste blood,
I can taste it pour out through the splintered cracks.
Inside beads upon beads of glimmering white
disappear into the hot thickness of it,
like a delirious sweating headache.
I imagine a hand over a neck,
holding the steady knife,
vein-threaded eyes staring out
terrified through the ancient doors.

Her calf smells the blood, the fear.
It smells the knife sliding
out of its mother's aged neck.
I watch her calf
while birds hysterically peck at my hands.

DAD SAVED IT TOO LATE

I stood there, in my white bathrobe,
and its grey figure lay on the kitchen sink,
spread over a water-stained sheet of paper.
Before I had discovered it, it seemed the mites had.
They crawled over its pointed rump.
And as I approached near the sink
a little head revealed itself from beneath
the yellow, protruding from the grey.
Its feet tucked under itself,
face turned to a side, away from me,
and wings slightly outstretched
as if it had fallen on its face mid-flight.

VULTURES

The hot air drenched my skin, my bare feet thumped against
the ground, the dry red dirt spread out before me and on
either side of me lay an expanse of dead yellow grass with
small islands of wheat fields that stood to attention beneath
the sun. In the distance circled dark clouds, they swirled low to
the ground held up by immense silky black wings, and where
the sun shone through their feathers streaks of metallic purple
glimmered.

Arms outstretched as we approached, leaping into the air
as we rushed forward, leaving behind the faint figures of
our mothers, who filled us with fear through stories of being
snatched away, and childish unknowing carried us into the eye
of the cloud, and we came face to face with the diseased raw
pink and black sticky carcass that the storm tore at.

AFTERNOONS

We were not accustomed to
the heat, unlike our cousins.
And it poured over us so that we breathed
beads of hotness through our skin
and tasted burnt dust on our tongues.

Here, the bare trees provided no shade,
and the silly afterthought barn attempted
to outstand the bubbling of the sun.

We strode on, branches trailing behind us;
restless with afternoon siestas,
the six of us headed out west,
towards the hills that cowered under the bulk of the Himalayas.
And we found a tree, bone-thin, drooping
in an eagerness to lie down.

Sharing its surprising strength
two at a time,
clambering over the dry brittle bark.
My cousin, tactfully moving the branches
out my way. Until I heaved myself up to his height,
and peered into a nest
and burrowed they lay there
freckled and unhatched,
Indian Ocean blue,
bright against the burning day.

DUBAI

You ask us to build
your skyscrapers.
You marvel at their ceilings
hidden in clouds.

Passportless, and without families,
instead we dream of Himalayas,
for our hands have seen the
heights of the heavens of this world.

VERINAG

FOETICIDE

You are the face of every woman that went before you.
You are the woman
who sliced the hands of Mughals.
You are the woman
who took up arms against the Raj.
You are the woman
that held the value of Kohi-Noor in her palms.
You are the woman in whose hands life itself is determined.

Yes, you carry on you the story
of every woman who went before you.
Yes, you carry within you the story
of every woman who is to come after you.

READYING

I grow,
I wait for you,
I ready myself.
I run fingers over your clothes.
The physical manifestations that you are.
That you will be.
I hold on to the dream that is you.
Gently pat, pat.
I walk through days as though asleep.
Sometimes a ghost, the world loses me.
I try to hold on to my growing body,
but I am in my mind too often.
A frenzy of to-do lists, preparations,
reality tumults around our togetherness.
I hold you within me,
I listen out for the movements of you,
my body awaiting your poking,
and nudgings, and bulgings.
Soundless, we speak to one another.
My footsteps, pat, pat,
shadowless, as I drift from room to room,
lists that haunt me in my sleep,
thoughts that escape me in my dreams.
Quiet anticipation,
the world opens itself up,
I notice things that were not before,
I am the consciousness of two,
I carve a space for you.
I ready myself,
I wait,
pat,
pat.

NESTING

And as I grow the world gets smaller,
eternal darknesses unfold,
I grow and
lights switch off.
Darkness expands and explodes,
dust fills up my lungs,
my breath catches,
I grow and the world gets smaller,
the thick dimness of the stars drowns me.
And the world turns around and closes itself from me.
And as I grow, roots take a hold of my spirit.
And I hoard heavy,
I collect galaxies in your wait,
gathering the formations of clouds,
I am sucked into their vortexes,
under the weight I tire,
my mind spirals through the world.
My arms outstretched,
my hands grabbing,
I grow, I prepare,
no rest,
I grow,
my mind unstill,
I bear down, I grow,
nothing is enough, I grow.
And all around me the world
keeps swallowing into itself.

SATI-SARAS

Quiet, quietly,
it creeps up on you,
at first you lean in to hear her.
Nestled between Pir Panjal,
she seems as still as
the black-necked crane,
adorned with the bobbing of lotus.
At first quiet.
Quietly.
She begins to gather momentum,
still the rush nothing but a gentle hum in the ear,
a thick wetness between the light of chinar leaves.
She builds up around you,
the undercurrents begin to pull you in,
the sounds steady, surround you,
yes, she shakes herself into you,
carries you along,
where stream meets river,
river to meet ocean.
She was never just quiet quietly.
She was always the still before the monsoon,
the calm before the delirium,
the steadiness that that carries cyclones
through your lands,
she is the truth that catches your breath.

She was never just quiet quietly.

OTHER WOMEN

I have always been too fat.

The way I could hold my skin
between my thumb and forefinger
would determine my day.
The disgust would sit heavy in me.
I would carry it around like a just punishment
for not looking like other women.

GRAVITY

Eyes that follow
you into your sleep.
Windowless.
I am no longer secret.

A heaviness has come
and sat above my brows.
The self-assurance
of my jawline
no longer holds my head high.

And still it watches me.
Pries truths from me.
My crown.
Panjnad.
Indus.
Each wave, curl, fold
is losing the night.
I am no longer sacred.
I reflect only
emptiness of moon.
My face is not
my face anymore.

Instead I hold on to the things
gravity cannot pull from me.

KISS

Nose,
a sword
of northern territories,
of grandmothers,
and great-grandmothers,
of Moghul painting.
It sits amidst wild hair,
not straight,
not curly.
Below eyes
that never
go to war
without *kajal.*
Above lips that
are not full,
not thin.
not of land,
not of sky,
but where the two meet
on the tip of Himalaya.
All flesh,
all skin,
all snow-capped,
ready to melt lakes and rivers.

SIX MONTHS

I awoke one night
with the overflowing urge to walk,
a longing to walk
and fill my pockets with stones,
rocks, the smoothness of pebbles
and walk
and keep adding heaviness to myself and walk
towards the stream that runs like madness
behind our home
and keep walking through the stream
until it reaches a weir,
to keep walking through that weir
until it becomes a gushing river
and keep walking through that gushing river
until it becomes an insane bubbling,
I wanted that cold frothing whiteness
to take me,
I wanted to breathe it all in.
There was a sigh caught in my throat
that I could not rid any other way.

GIRL

We waited for clouds to flower
into existence and submerge our parched lives.
The heat was unusually early for the time of year.
Not your usual heat.
This heat made your skin open up,
and wait.
Our eyes watched for clouds,
hairs on the back of our neck ready in anticipation.
Sweat beads halted in their path.
Our entire body waited.
Too early the crops bowed under the weight of the sky.
The insects chirped insanely that spring
and the mosquitos grew fat.
You made me tired.
The sun didn't help.
I wanted to curl under the shade of the trees
with the cats that switched off to the world.
You made me ache.
I've never felt such a sense of myself before.
Marrow. Bone. Muscle. Tendons. Veins.
Rib cage. Skin. My entire body waiting for you.
You would be two weeks late.
It was the night that the clouds flowered,
and rain bombarded into our parched lives,
and under the strong light of the moon
you came onto our world.
Oblivious, the farmers rushed
about their fields
in busy excitement,
preparing to tunnel life into withering roots.

And it struck me then that the world would be cruel to you.
I understood why I was pitied.
You are my daughter.
And I must protect you
against a world that burns after you.

SONSHINE

My warm flesh wrapped
around my son's sleeping figure.
The feel of his woolly head under my stroke.
The wrinkle of his eyelids under the dim light
that scatters our room,
we wrapped in each other,
him asleep, little ear pressed
to the steady beat of my heart.
I awake watching the rise and fall
of his birdcage chest.
My son radiates shine that consumes me,
and at times we are one.
And when I wake in the night
on the verge of my sleep
and his dream feeds,
my exhaustion borderlines euphoria and back again.
And it is at this precise moment in time
that all the well-meaning and good-intentioned
bullshit advice falls, slips and slides
away from the ache in my lower back,
the soreness between my shoulder blades,
the tenderness of my breasts,
the tiredness of my eyes,
the swollenness of my womb.
And disappears into the shadows of nooks and crannies.

And I watch my son sleep,
I watch him radiate shine,
I watch his little figure breathe in and out,
in the dim light of our hibernation.

RIVER JHELUM

LOSS

It was a night when trees collected light into their limbs
and scattered shadows onto our world.
Under the crashing clouds
that sucked yellow moonbeams into their dense bodies.

The night dew exploded under our feet,
while we avoided the crowd up ahead
as it wobbled over cobbled streets,
laughter ricocheting into empty spaces,
vying against the drunken click of stilettos.

And in the cacophony of a Friday night
you hold my hand,
the way you hold my hand
tells me so much about you.
The way your energy
runs through my fingers
and explodes in my chest.
And tonight you hold on to me tight,
and we walk like that, hand in hand,
you pressing your pain into my palm.
Hands swinging heavy between us.
Knuckles white, fingers entwined,
hand in hand.

Thoughts unknown to me
but dangerous like ripples,
memories the splurge of bubbles,
pain that is deep and green and jagged.
And you float there.
You're lost to me.
And I try to hold on to you,
I wait for you to come back to me.

And with every breath I take,
I wish I can take your pain in through my palm,
and push it deep into the pit of my stomach.
So that you can be free,
so that you would no longer clam up
at the memory of it,

but open up like my palm,
heal up like a scar.

And we walk like that,
hand in hand,
and in the shadows,
under the burning night,
and in the silence,
I pray for you.

NOW

Like so many years before,
we are snaking through winding streets,
this time we walk arm in arm.
Except that now we talk about streetlights,
our roads look unfamiliar in the night.
We step over awkward truths,
we do not talk about betrayals,
and drunk on the darkness
we breathe in the cold night air,
deep into our throats,
and instead of dreams,
mist spills out from our mouths
and rests into the darkness of night.

We do not speak of forevers and never-agains,
we do not conjure up the future like the lovers we once were.
We do not speak about starlight,
but only of the darkness,
those without hope,
the streetlights,
the addicts,
the now.

HUSH

We drove uphill steadily,
heading towards home.
The day drew to a close,
and the warm May night
accompanied us, while we
weaved through blue fields.
No stars peered down on us,
and silence carried us forward.
While we, with sleepy eyes and through
yawns, spoke reminiscent thoughts,
pondered on what we didn't have
and hoped when we should not have.
And we approached the top of the hill,
and synchronised around a bend,
home shone out at us,
neon lights glimmered
like static fireflies,
they spread out before us,
an immense lake that
glided through blue soundless fields.
And we dipped into its silence.

SONG

The melodies swung around us,
rhythms that swayed the room,
the quick pace of the percussion,
the dim lighting.
And we sat, far at the back.
While the voice of the oud sprang out at us,
toyed with our memories,
spoke to the audience in words unknown to our ears.

Entranced, necks craned,
ready to witness the dazzle of hands,
accents thick and luscious,
falling over rows of bobbing heads,
nimble fingers fled across string,
plucking journeys out into the air.
A hurricane let loose,
it drunkenly swayed its way across the room,
oozing sounds that vibrated through the walls
and staggered onto the pavement outside,
making its escape through the night-startled traffic.

And all the while,
I sat, pulled in close to you,
with your heart beating in my ear,
a song for only me to hear.

FIVE

You, my son with five rivers
under your skin,
complexion the colour of this dark universe,
will come to know that we stand by you,
will come to learn how to follow
in the footsteps of our prophets.
To follow the flow of the Jhelum.
You will come to know the first,
like the Shahada,
that we believe in you.
Like the second,
Selah,
we will hold your name
on our lips in *duas*.
Like the third,
Zakat,
we will be there for you
in your times of need.
Like the fourth,
Ramadan,
from dawn to the hours of darkness,
your actions will bring to life the sacred;
we live in times of revelations, my son.
Like the fifth,
Hajj,
like the pilgrim,
like a mother,
like your father
we intend to journey this world over,
to find your place in it.
Dismantling borders,
gathering with our *Ummah*,
to remember ourselves,
every footstep and reflection of our faith,
every word of every prayer
triggering a memory,
reminding us of our prophet,
reminding us of your future.

Know, my son,
like the five,
we stand by you.

ROLE MODELS

Our son heavy under the weight of our prayers,
five rivers running under his skin,
goes into the world.
We teach him
his skin is to be worn with a proudness.
He is people of mountains,
courage is the make-up of their skin.
While primary school questionnaires,
lying in wait like paper snakes,
tick boxes looking for signs of dissent,
we remind him he is more than the here and now.
We plan futures for you, my son,
we hold to the stories of your everyday courage.
Know we stand by you,
even on days when I despair,
days that look like Malcolm,
Mangal Pandey, Ghandi.
You, my son, are not
just given role models,
but martyrs.

You, my son heavy under the weight of our prayers,
five rivers running under your skin,
go into the world.

REMEMBER, MY DAUGHTER

Remember, my daughter,
remember, when you find yourself bookended
between images of women with gold glittering hair
who advertise desire
and speak to those who have the ability to obtain.
Remember, my daughter,
when you see those images of paper-thin women
dying a slow death, gold hair glittering.
That you come from a long line of strong women,
bodies hard, childbearing,
reflecting the beauty of your brown skin.
You, my child, will not always be Miss Universes and Miss Worlds.
You are the universe itself,
you encompass within you the beauty of navigators.
Across lands, under stars and over seas,
this world belongs to you.
We are the children of migrants
browned and dark-eyed,
we've marked the world with footsteps speaking of our journeying.
So mark this world with your presence,
not with thigh gaps and the ability to disappear
but in a homage to your foremothers
through stretch marks on real skin.

So remember when you find yourself bookended
between images of women with gold glittering hair,
who epitomise desire and the ability to obtain,
that no, you will not find your identity on that TV screen.
But understand where you belong,
not as a Miss World or a Miss Universe,
but as a woman to whom the world belongs.
You can navigate this earth with the wisdom of a nomad,
feel this earth deep down in your bones
and you will find yourself amongst the stars and galaxies.
You have been given the gift to carve your own destiny,
so choose to belong to something far greater
than what can ever be depicted
within the rigid confines of this society
and that small box that babbles away ceaselessly into empty evenings.
You, my child, will speak worlds into creation,
you are the universe itself and every beauty it has ever glimmered
   into hope.

RIVER CHENAB

SKIN

It is not that I do not want
to wear my skin anymore.
But it is because I am more
than just my darkness.
Sometimes,
I just want to rest,
to switch off,
my skin,
your gaze.

EMPIRE

I was doing alright.
Until I met him.
Needy, complicated.
Full of drama.
It was small man syndrome.
It was upbringing.
He was misunderstood.
He was island.
Needed to be given a chance.

Everyone said he would be cruel.
But it happened so slow.
And then suddenly it was
two hundred years of sorrow
that sat into my bones,
into the salt of me.

I had let him hold
my face in his hands.
Whisper in my ears.
Let him mute the spice of me.
He slipped heirlooms off my nakedness,
fingers, neck, wrists, ankles exposed.
Put his dick into the soil of me.

I bore the children he denied.
He drew lines across my body,
broke me into nationless pieces,
gave me a blade,
sat and watched
blood flow.
He waited for me to become all teeth and nails and bones.

POPPY FIELDS AND CEDAR TREES

*Beirut has often been referred to as the Paris
of the Middle East.*

On Sunday we remembered,
on Sunday we said never again,
lest we forget.
On Monday it was noted
that bows were not bowed enough.
That chests, red robin, were not proud enough.
On Tuesday we sold a £4 billion arms deal to Saudi Arabia.
Silence. 11am.
On Wednesday we held our breath.
On Thursday, quietly, invisibly Beirut fell.
On Friday Paris too fell.
On Saturday refugees
ambushed by borders,
swallowed by seas,
were compared to rodents.

Fascism was never really defeated.
We would soon be at war.
We are good at war.

On Saturday my head is heavy.
On Sunday I need air.
On Sunday I walk through woods with my children.
We want to colour our hands with the redness of poppies.
Behind us we do not hear the fall of a cedar tree.

REVOLUTION

When the revolution starts,
when the revolution rolls itself
through our streets full force.
Maybe because we are mothers, and your lovers,
we know how to stand like in Selah,
shoulder to shoulder,
always behind you,
row upon row gathering strength.

And when we are called upon.
When justice is not done.
And when 'prevent' is used to silence you.
When the brownness of your skin is
reason enough for violence against you.
We drop ourselves to give voice to you,
speak out for your cause,
because your cause is our cause.

But when the revolution is done.
When the revolution is finished.
Our names are forgotten in *duas*.
Our voices get silenced.
Sidelined.
Forgotten.
We go back to being just *aurat*.
Awrah.
Lips in the wrong place.

Because when the revolution is done.
When the revolution is won.
The revolution forgets it was meant for everyone.

HISTORY

When we first arrived,
you sent us yourself not in letters,
but cassette tapes.
We listen to them still.
To us this is what pharaoh left behind
in the shape of pyramids and Sphinx.
Greek columns,
the ruins of Jerusalem,
broken tiles mosaicing
together memories of Saladin.
This is history.
Our history.
Your voice,
not just from cobwebbed decades ago,
but right here and right now.
Towering over us,
your voice in all its vivaciousness
bursting through the walls of our terraced homes.
Bring back to life what we left to fade.

POTWARI

Too often,
I choke on the words,
they hang heavy in the air.
I struggle to recall you
through your own language,
a language that we should share.

There are times when
I've lost the story of you,
your script hovers in my throat,
tugs at my heart,
the sense of you sits
in the pit of my stomach,
but I cannot speak you.
Instead get caught on you.
It is getting even harder to imagine you.

RIVER PANJNAD

PRAYER

There are moments of prayer
that have imprinted themselves
not only on my lips
but on somewhere in the depths of my memories.
A time when sunbeams shone through *Jummah* prayers
like geometric patterns of Jami al Kutibiyyah
where the remnants of French colonisation
live on side by side
with the footprints of the Toureg Berber tribe,
and the heavens and skies illuminate blues on Chefchaouen.
It is here that I bowed my head before Allah
and offered up my prayer,
side by side,
my recitation echoed back
by the soft voice of a young girl beside me.
Never has prayer held so much power as it did
when whispered by the innocent faith of a child.
And I was reminded of hope.
And I am reminded of a time
where once in the heart of Paris
shielded by minaret and secret trees
a Great Mosque acted as a place of refuge
for our Jewish family.
I am reminded of Lassana Bathily,
and those frightened bodies
shivering in a fridge,
power off,
lights off,
hoping on.
I am reminded of an image,
two women side by side
and that yellow burning star
blanketed over by the bravery of friendships.
And it is these acts of humanity
that remind us there is always hope.
And every time I pray
I remember both the Mishna and the Qur'an teach us,
'Whoever destroys a single life
it is as though he had destroyed the entire world,
and whoever saves a single life

it is as if he had saved the entire world.'
And side by side I pray
and I continue to hope.

RIVER INDUS

WITCH

The first witch was an ancestor of mine.
It wasn't green skin, but brown that she wore.
Her nose a *talwar*,
her cackle the earthiness of Punjab.

She used too many spices for you.
Her prayer would put a fear in you.
Her customs too strange for you.

So you wanted to drown her,
send her back to those five rivers.
That skin of hers, all sun and earth,
you wanted to see what water would do with it.

EMPIRE II

He did not know
I am made up of flow,
I am Jhelum, Chenab, Ravi, Beas, Sutlej.

GLOSSARY

Ummah

Islamic term for the brotherhood/sisterhood of Islam

Parandeh

Hair accessory that ties into braids, worn by South Asian women

Nare

Informal term for the river Jhelum, meaning 'river'

Um

Mango

Bare

Berry

Sootan

Trouser

Khuchi

Underwear

Niat

Intention

Li la ha illil la ho Muhammad ar rasullila

There is no god but Allah, and Muhammad is the messenger of Allah

Bismillah ah rahman neera heem

In the name of the most merciful, the most kind

Inshallah

God willing

Kaleh Phar

Black mountains

Alhamdo Lillahi Rabbil Aalameen Ar Rahmaanir Raheem Maaliki Yaomid Deen iyya Kana Budoo Wa iyya kanastaeen ihdinas Siratual Mustaqeem Siratual Lazeena An Amtaa Alaihim Ghairil Maghdoobe Alaihim Walad Dualleen Ameen

The Compassionate, the Merciful.
Lord of the Day of Judgement.
You alone we worship,

and to You alone we pray for help.
Guide us to the straight path.
The path of those whom You have favoured
Not of those who have incurred Your wrath,
nor of those who have gone astray.

Potawri

Punjabi dialect

Goriya veh

White-skinned

Jissam

Body

Aurat aur pani na keh farq

What difference between the body of water and the body of a woman

Qurbani

Sacrifice

Shahada

Testimony or witness (first pillar of Islam)

Selah

Five daily prayers (second pillar of Islam)

Dua

Prayer

Zakat

Charity (third pillar of Islam)

Ramadan

Month of fasting (fourth pillar of Islam)

Hajj

Pilgrimage to Mecca (fifth pillar of Islam)

Aurat

Woman (Urdu), derived from Arabic

Awrah

Intimate parts of the body

Jummah

Friday

ACKNOWLEDGEMENTS

This book is dedicated to all the women in my family, past, present and future. It is dedicated to the strength and wisdom of my mother and my sisters. It is dedicated to the memory of my grandmothers and great-grandmothers. I write for my daughter, who faces the world with a courage so divine, so life-affirming that I am inspired every day by her. I write for my son, who encompasses both the masculine and the feminine in an unashamedly sensitive and emotionally intelligent way. I am proud and honoured to be their mother. And I'd like to thank Imran for his support and for always believing in my work.

My poetic journey could not have taken the path it has if it were not for the encouragement and support of the Bristol Black Writers, Edson Burton, Bertel Martin, Glenn Carmichael, Lucy English, Annie McGann, Sharon Clarke, Kate Offord, Gina Sherman, Lucy Lepchani, Rebecca Tantony, Elizabeth K Mizon, Amani Z Saeed, Shareefa Energy, Afshan Lodhi, Shruti Chauhan, Anjali Barot, Naylah Ahmed, Tanuja Amarasuriya, Zeba Talkani, Helen Mott, Michal Nahman, Sian Norris, and the many people who have given me the platforms and opportunities to keep at the writing game.

I would like to thank my publisher Burning Eye Books, Clive Birnie, Jenn Hart, Liv Torc, and Harriet Evans, who have made this poet's dream come true. Finally, a special mention to the amazing artist that is Angela Aujla, who created the cover art.

.

The Road Chose Me
http://theroadchoseme.com

This The Road Chose Me paperback edition published 2020
1 3 5 7 9 10 8 6 4 2

A catalogue record for this book is available from Archives Canada

ISBN 978-0-9951989-6-8

Cover & logo design by Bari Simon
http://bazzavisualdesign.com

Cover Photograph Copyright© 2017 Dan Grec
Democratic Republic of Congo

All photographs Copyright© 2015-2019 Dan Grec

Join Dan's ongoing global adventures at
http://theroadchoseme.com

ALSO BY DAN GREC